PAULINE PREDESTINATION

by

The Rev. FRANCIS DAVIDSON, M.A., B.D., D.D.

Formerly Professor of Old Testament and New Testament Language and Literature, United Original Secession Church of Scotland and Principal of the Bible Training Institute, Glasgow.

LONDON

THE TYNDALE PRESS

THE TYNDALE NEW TESTAMENT LECTURE, 1945

The Lecture was delivered on January 3rd, 1946, at a Conference of graduate and theological student members of the Inter-Varsity Fellowship, in the Old Combination Room, Trinity College, Cambridge.

Printed in Great Britain by
Green & Co. (Lowestoft) Ltd., Crown Street, Lowestoft.

PAULINE PREDESTINATION

T HE doctrine of predestination is Pauline only in the one supreme sense, that it fell to the lot of the great apostle to the Gentiles to develop it to its height. It is a mistake to think that Paul originated the doctrine, or wandered into a by-path of revelation, as he matured its truth. The Rabbi of Tarsus inherited the very spirit of the doctrine from the history and teaching of his race. The Old Testament Scriptures are infused with the breath of the sovereignty of almighty God, who is so exalted as the first cause in His own universe, that second causes are of immaterial account. God is in intimate contact with all events, and nothing lies outwith His holy and wise control. Every happening is the expression of the divine will. The ' voice of the Lord ' is heard on land and sea and in the sky, ' the Lord sitteth King for ever ' (Ps. 29). The prophet, like the Psalmist, is equally God-conscious and even dares to postulate the emergence of evil to the all-embracing and absolute will of God. ' Shall there be evil in a city, and the Lord hath not done it ?' (Am. 3 : 6). It is so in the warp and woof of the Old Testament writings, all of which were the heritage of the apostle Paul.

This same sense of sovereignty is found in the teaching of Jesus, which only those who ignore the historical origin of Christianity would deny to the converted Saul of Tarsus. The same Lord who arrested this anguished seeker after righteousness made His mind clear to His chosen vessel. There are some challenging words that can never be lightly thrust aside and which must have entered into the soul of Paul, as into well-prepared soil. ' All that the Father giveth me shall come to me; and him that cometh to me I will in no wise cast out.' ' No man can come to me, except the Father which hath sent me draw him : and I will raise him up at the last day.' ' My sheep hear my voice, and I know them, and they follow me : and I give unto them eternal life; and they shall never perish, neither shall any man pluck them out of my hand. My Father, which gave them me, is greater than all; and no man is able to pluck them out of my Father's hand.' ' Holy Father, keep through

3

thine own name those whom thou hast given me, that they may be one, as we are . . . Those that thou gavest me I have kept, and none of them is lost, but the son of perdition,' ὁ υἱὸς τῆς ἀπωλείας (Jn. 6: 37, 44; 10: 27-29; 17: 11, 12).

However much or little is granted to the apostle as his legacy from Hebrew revelation and the mind of Christ, it is agreed that Paul, above others, is the exponent of the doctrine of predestination. It is proposed here to deal with the Pauline vocabulary, the Pauline context, the Pauline doctrine as derived from both vocabulary and context, and briefly to append some thoughts inspired by later interpretations of Paul's mind.

THE PAULINE VOCABULARY

There are a few key words which the apostle uses directly in stating the doctrine of predestination and which are worthy of scrutiny.

1. προορίζω. πρό, before, and ὁρίζω whose root is ὅρος, a boundary, hence to mark off beforehand. The term occurs six times, all of which save one (Acts 4: 28) are Pauline (Rom. 8: 29, 30; 1 Cor. 2: 7; Eph. 1: 5, 11). The Authorized Version translated all Paul's words but one (1 Cor. 2: 7, ordain) by the term predestinate. According to Abbott-Smith (p. 382) the compound is not found in the LXX or other Greek Versions of the Old Testament and Apocrypha, or in Greek writers of the classical period. In the face of the fact that Luke uses the word as he reports the prayer of the primitive Church (Acts 4: 28, ' determined before ') it would be venturesome to say that Paul coined the term, but obviously the compound is a genuine Christian dictum. This appears more emphatically since the other New Testament compound ἀφορίζω, separate, is a classical and Septuagint term, while διορίζω, divide, is classical but not New Testament.

The Vulgate renders προορίζω by praedestinatio (except Acts 4: 28, decerno) from which we get our English word, predestination. Beza uses praedefinio in Acts 4: 28 and 1 Corinthians 2: 7, but praedestinatio in the other cases.

Cremer (p. 462) observes, ' The matter to be considered, when the word is used, is not *who* are the objects of the Predestination but *what* they are predestined to. The second object of the verb forms an essential part of the conception expressed by it: what is called the first object, *i.e.* the persons who, is an accidental one, a contingency belonging to history, whereas προορίζω itself precedes history.' Cremer gives the honours to προγίνώσκω, *foreknow*, as a complete and independent conception in itself.

2. προγινώσκω, *foreknow*. This word appears in the New Testament as the verb only five times and as the noun πρόγνωσις only twice (Acts 26: 5; Rom. 8: 29; 11: 2; 1 Pet. 1: 20; 2 Pet. 3: 17; Acts 2: 23; 1 Pet. 1: 2; Moulton and Geden, p. 851). Hence Paul uses only the verb and that but twice, in Romans 8: 29 and 11: 2.

The simple term γινώσκω, whose content Paul predicates to God before the foundations of the earth in the far-off eternity, implies a self-reference of the knower to the known, an active relation of cognition. It differs from οἶδα whose object merely comes within the sphere of perception; *e.g.* the words of Matthew 25: 12, οὐκ οἶδα ὑμᾶς, have the meaning *you stand in no relation to me*. The synonyms of the noun (*vide* Trench, p. 281) emphasize the conscious relationship between subject and object as being the special contribution of γνῶσις. Σοφία is *sapientia*, wisdom primary and absolute; φρόνησις is *prudentia*, prudence or practical wisdom; σύνεσις is *intelligentia*, understanding or critical wisdom; but γνῶσις is *cognitio*, that knowledge which involves personal contact, if not communion. God accordingly foreknows or *can enter into relation with* persons, even before they are born. Moulton and Milligan, however, referring to 1 Peter 1: 2, state that, while the foreknowledge is of a person, it is not so much in relation to himself as to his function.

3. ἐκλέγω, ἐκλεκτός, ἐκλογή. The verb in the New Testament is used only in the middle voice ' to choose for oneself ', and of its twenty-one times Paul employs it only four times (Eph. 1: 4; 1 Cor. 1: 27 (twice), 28). The adjective ἐκλεκτός-η-ον appears twenty-four times, of which the apostle uses it six times (Rom. 8: 33; 16: 13; Col. 3: 12; 1 Tim. 5: 21; 2 Tim. 2: 10; Tit. 1: 1). The noun ἐκλογή is used by Paul five times out of its seven occurrences (*viz.* Rom. 9: 11; 11: 5, 7, 28; 1 Thes. 1: 4) and

always of the divine choice.   In Romans 9: 11 and 11: 28, it is
unqualified as free choice, while in 11 : 5 we have ἐκλογὴ χάριτος,
election of grace; and in 1 Thessalonians 1 : 4, ἐκλογὴ ὑμῶν, *your
election.*   Romans 11 : 7 gives us ἡ ἐκλογή equal to οἱ ἐκλεκτοί, *the
elect themselves.*

ἐκλέγω is a LXX term and translates the Hebrew בָּחַר which
associates the idea of *testing* with that of *choice, e.g.* Isaiah 48:
10, ' Behold, I have refined thee, but not with silver; I have
chosen thee in the furnace of affliction (RV mg., *tried*).'   B.D.B.,
p. 104, notes ' I have tested thee in the furnace of affliction.
בְּחַרְתִּיךָ בְּכוּר עֹנִי ' but this is the only case where the idea
protrudes.   It is far from certain that the Greek ἐκλέγω, the New
Testament equivalent to בָּחַר, carries anything of this conception
of proving with it.   On the contrary, its usage is that of simple,
free choice.   The noun בָּחִיר is always of divine choice and is
the exact synonym of ἐκλογή, the elect of God.   (1 Ch. 16: 13;
Pss. 89: 3; 105: 6, 43; 106: 5, 23; Is. 42: 1; 43: 20; 45: 4;
65: 9, 15, 22.)   Vg. *electi.*

4.   κλητός, √καλέω, *to call.*   (LXX for קָרָא.)   In the New
Testament it refers always to the divine call, both to office and
to salvation; of the seven Pauline instances, five refer to spiritual
status, as apostleship or sainthood, and two to spiritual deliverance
in Christ (Rom. 1: 1, 6, 7; 1 Cor. 1: 1, 2; Rom. 8: 28; 1 Cor.
1: 24).   The Gospel of Matthew (20: 16; 22: 14) distinguishes between ' the called ' and ' the chosen ' — πολλοὶ γάρ εἰσιν κλητοί,
ὀλίγοι δὲ ἐκλεκτοί.   The root verb καλέω is a favourite term of
Paul and largely used of naming and of inviting into the privileges
of the kingdom of God.   Cremer (pp. 330 ff.) has a helpful note on
the noun, κλῆσις, which, according to Moulton and Geden
(p. 550), occurs chiefly in Paul, nine times out of the eleven New
Testament instances, the other two being Hebrews 3: 1 and
2 Peter 1: 10 (Rom. 11: 29; 1 Cor. 1: 26; 7: 20; Eph. 1: 18;
4: 1, 4; Phil. 3: 14; 2 Thes. 1: 11; 2 Tim. 1: 9).   ' The κλῆσις is
the first act towards the realization of the divine election (cf. 1
Cor. 1: 26, 27) and the called must make it secure, 2 Pet. 1: 10,
σπουδάσατε βεβαίαν ὑμῶν τὴν κλῆσιν καὶ ἐκλογὴν ποιεῖσθαι.

Partly on account of the subject ἡ κλῆσις τοῦ Θεοῦ (Rom. 11 : 29), and partly on account of end and aim, ἐλπὶς τῆς κλήσεως (Eph. 1 : 18; 4 : 4), it is termed in Philippians 3 : 14, ἡ ἄνω κλῆσις, the vocation which bears the character of the world above, of the supramundane and heavenly; cf. Hebrews 3 : 1, κλήσεως ἐπουρανίου μέτοχοι the calling whose origin, nature, and goal are heavenly. In 2 Timothy 1 : 9, it is termed ἁγία because it proceeds from God and is opposed to the sinful habitus of man : hence those who are called are required ἀξίως περιπατεῖν τῆς κλήσεως (Eph. 4 : 1; cf. 2 Thes. 1 : 11).' It is noted by Moulton and Milligan, ' The way is prepared for New Testament usage by the mention of the " guests " (οἱ κλητοί) of Adonijah in 1 Kings 1 : 41, 49.' It is also suggested that οἱ κλητοί, as distinguished from οἱ κεκλημένοι, denotes that the call has been obeyed.

5. προτίθημι, to set before, in Mid. to set before oneself, to purpose. The verb is found only in Paul (Rom. 1 : 13; 3 : 25; Eph. 1 : 9). The noun πρόθεσις occurs in the Gospels with the meaning of publicly setting forth (Mt. 12 : 4; Mk. 2 : 26; Lk. 6 : 4; and also Heb. 9 : 2). Paul uses πρόθεσις in its meaning of purpose in Romans 8 : 28; 9 : 11; Ephesians 1 : 11; 3 : 11; 2 Timothy 1 : 9; 3 : 10, the only other New Testament usages in this sense being Acts 11 : 23; 27 : 13. Deissmann confines his notes to the LXX usage as a ' setting forth ', especially in the phrase οἱ ἄρτοι τῆς προθέσεως i.e. the shewbread. (Bible Studies, p. 157.)

6. The three volitional terms employed by Paul, βουλή, θέλημα and εὐδοκία, are interesting.

Βουλή is the firm term for will, denoting the determined purpose of God, but Paul uses it sparingly, twice in his speeches recorded in Acts (13 : 36; 20 : 27), and once only in the Epistles (Eph. 1 : 11). He prefers θέλημα τοῦ Θεοῦ to βουλή τοῦ Θεοῦ, using it in his Epistles nineteen times. Once he writes τὸ θέλημα τοῦ Κυρίου. Θέλημα gives a bigger background to will in the divine character than βουλή and the usage is significant. That θέλημα is the larger conception, is revealed in his phrase κατὰ τὴν βουλὴν τοῦ θελήματος αὐτοῦ (Eph. 1 : 11).

Εὐδοκία, the seeming fit and proper, or the good pleasure, is used in the New Testament only nine times, and six of the instances are Pauline (Mt. 11 : 26; Lk. 2 : 14; 10 : 21; Rom. 10 : 1;

Eph. 1: 5, 9; Phil. 1: 15; 2: 13; 2 Thes. 1: 11), but only four
refer to the divine good pleasure. Again in combination θέλημα
hold its superior place (Eph. 1: 5, κατὰ τὴν εὐδοκίαν τοῦ θελήματος
αὐτοῦ).

THE PAULINE CONTEXT

a. 2 Thessalonians 2: 13, 14

Here the apostle is very definite about *the choice* — εἵλατο ὑμᾶς ὁ
Θεός — as a reality experienced by the Thessalonians in time,
although made in eternity — ἀπ' ἀρχῆς, a phrase which elsewhere
is expanded beyond doubt as to its pre-temporal meaning. The
realization in time of the eternal act of choice is affirmed to
take place in the gospel call, εἰς ὃ καὶ ἐκάλεσεν ὑμᾶς διὰ τοῦ
εὐαγγελίου ἡμῶν. Hence, the precedence of the *choice before the
call* must be noted, the call being the sequence of the choice both
in thought and time. The end of both choice and call is plainly
set forth—εἰς σωτηρίαν ἐν ἁγιασμῷ Πνεύματος καὶ πίστει ἀληθείας
— unto salvation environed and secured within the Spirit's
sanctifying operation and the soul's trusting acceptance of the
truth. Both the divine and the human activities, which guarantee
salvation, are closely knit together by the one preposition ἐν
signifying that both the Spirit's ministry and human faith are
essential and complementary to each other.

b. 2 Timothy 1: 9

The meaning of salvation is expounded by the co-ordinating and
epexegetical καὶ — who saved us, *i.e.* who called us with a holy
calling, the ground of which was not any works of merit on our
part, but simply the divine πρόθεσις, *purpose* or *plan*, which is
linked here with χάρις, *grace*, implying a purpose of grace, a
gracious manifestation, or display, of the divine character in our
direction, a goodwill, moreover, bestowed upon us *in Christ*,
ἐν Χριστῷ, before the temporal ages, or as Paul phrases it elsewhere, ἀπ' ἀρχῆς, *from the beginning*.

c. Ephesians 1: 1-12

This section of the circular letter which, it is believed, the apostle
addressed to more churches than Ephesus, has been described
as ' the whole ideal history of salvation in Christ from eternity

to eternity ', wherein are traced consecutively salvation's preparation (verses 4, 5), execution (verses 6, 7), publication (verses 8-10)
and application to both Jews and Gentiles (verses 11-14). 'Thus,
there is kept steadily before our eyes the wheel within wheel
of the all-comprehending decrees of God; first of all, the inclusive
cosmical purpose in accordance with which the universe is
governed, as it is led to its destined end; within this the purpose
relative to the Kingdom of God, a substantive part and, in some
sort, the hinge of the world-purpose itself; and, still within this,
the purpose of grace, relative to the individual, by virtue of which
he is called into the Kingdom and made sharer in its blessings:
the common element with them all being that they are come to
pass only in accordance with the good pleasure of God's will.'
(Prof. Warfield, *H.D.B.*, Vol. iii, p. 60.)

Here again is the pre-mundane note for the divine choice
καθὼς ἐξελέξατο ἡμᾶς ἐν αὐτῷ (ἐν Χριστῷ) πρὸ καταβολῆς κόσμου
— *before the pitching of the universe.* This is Paul's idea of the
choice fixed definitely in its non-time setting. The end of this
eternal election is just as plain — εἶναι ἡμᾶς ἁγίους καὶ ἀμώμους
κατενώπιον αὐτοῦ — *that we be holy and blameless in His presence.* The predestination, which here is the outcome of the
blessed election, runs to the same transforming redemptive goal
— προορίσας ἡμᾶς εἰς υἱοθεσίαν διὰ Ἰησοῦ Χριστοῦ εἰς αὐτόν —
*having predestined us for sonship with Himself as Father, through
Jesus Christ.*

The source of the whole election and foreordination is distinctly
stated to be, in verse 5, 'the good pleasure of his will', κατὰ
τὴν εὐδοκίαν τοῦ θελήματος αὐτοῦ, and in verse 11, 'the purpose
of him who worketh all things after the counsel of his own will'—
κατὰ πρόθεσιν τοῦ τὰ πάντα ἐνεργοῦντος κατὰ τὴν βουλὴν τοῦ
θελήματος αὐτοῦ. In this statement of the origin of predestination *Paul uses all his three terms,* βουλή, εὐδοκία and θέλημα,
and both will and good-pleasure are used as parts of the larger
conception, θέλημα, the divine disposition, which is at once intel-
lectual and emotional, as well as volitional.

d.   Romans 8: 28-30
The atmosphere of this passage is one of designed encouragement

to all readers in Rome who were perturbed with the uncertainties
of life and especially with the parlous position of the Christian
in that chaotic age.   The strange providences of life are not the
changeful products of chance or fate, but the events of an ordered
government by the God and Father of our Lord Jesus Christ.   All
that occurs has the stamp of divine purposefulness, κατὰ πρόθεσιν,
according to express plan, an outline of which is given in five
steps — προέγνω, προώρισεν, ἐκάλεσεν, ἐδικαίωσεν, ἐδόξασεν —
foreknowledge, predestination, calling, justification and *glorification*.   As we noted in discussing the Pauline vocabulary, this idea
of foreknowledge implies personal contact, relationship, or communion, and is, therefore, the appropriate fountain-head of the
subsequent activities of God in relation to the elect.   This is
frequently referred to as the *pregnant sense* of the term πρόγνωσις
as distinguished from the sense of ' merely contemplative foresight ', which issues in nothing actual.   Cremer (p. 161) takes
προγινώσκω to mean *unite oneself before with someone*, rendering
Romans 11 : 2, ' God has not cast away his people, with whom
he had before joined himself,' *i.e.* a union, before any union was
historically realized.   Similarly here, in Romans 8 : 29, ' whom
God had beforehand entered into fellowship with, he also predestinated.'   Prof. K. E. Kirk (*Clarendon Bible*, p. 120), while not
predicating so close a relationship as communion to the verb
προέγνω, nevertheless states the meaning in pregnant terms.
' The distinction between " foreknew " and " foreordained " is
not at all clear, though the former evidently represents an earlier
stage in the divine purpose than the latter.   Probably S. Paul is
using an anthropomorphic metaphor in an attempt to emphasize
the overwhelming graciousness of God's love towards Christians.
In that case, " foreknew " means " cast His eyes upon them with
a view to conferring special favour upon them "; and " foreordained ", " decided that the favour should take the shape of
causing them to be conformed to the image of His Son."   Such a
discrimination between the two words gives to " foreknowledge "
a sense closely bound up with the biblical use of the word
γιγνώσκειν " to know " (*cf.* 1 Cor. 8 : 3; Gal. 4 : 9; Mt. 7 : 23;
Jn. 10 : 27; Pss. 1 : 6; 144 : 3; Ho. 13 : 5; Am. 3 : 2).'
    Foreknowledge is thus *dynamic* not *static*, and is the prolific

origin of subsequent activities, whose direction is towards the uplift of man. The second step προώρισεν conveys a divine movement towards man equally with προέγνω pre-temporal or timeless. Here we have predestination in its logical and eternal setting. Notice is to be taken of the second accusative, the 'what' as well as the 'who' of foreordination — συμμόρφους τῆς εἰκόνος τοῦ υἱοῦ αὐτοῦ. The foreknown are also *foreordained conformists* with the image of God's Son: their destiny is likeness to Christ.

The third step, ἐκάλεσεν, is the first act of God in time to fulfil the preceding foreknowledge and foreordination. Naturally it is the awakening, in those already predestined, to God's love-relation to them. After this 'gospel and grace call' come the divine acts of justification and glorification to perfect the saving purpose and relationship.

e. Romans 9-11

This section of Romans is suggested by C. H. Dodd (*Moffatt New Testament Commentary*, pp. 148 ff.) to be originally a treatise by itself, which Paul often used to defend the divine purpose in history, and for which he found a fitting place in his Epistle to the Romans. It deals with the problem of the rejection of the Jews, in face of the fact of their election to be the channel of revelation to the whole Gentile world, and also in face of such operation witnessed in the past. Amongst the many scholars who have helped to throw light upon this difficult passage, Professor A. B. Bruce is one of the most lucid (*St. Paul's Conception of Christianity*). He traces the trend of its thought thus: ' Paul deals with the hard problem in two ways, in both of which he successfully escapes the dreaded inference that his gospel is illegitimate. First, he reckons with the facts of the assumption that they signify an absolute final cancelling of Israel's election, striving to show that even in that case there is no presumption against his gospel, the argument of his opponents being: " If you are right in your view of Christianity, then God has rejected His chosen people, but such a rejection is impossible, therefore you are wrong." His reply, in the first instance, is, " Such a rejection is not impossible ".'

This is the argument in Romans 9 and 10, wherein Paul makes three points:

(1) There was always an election within the election (9: 6-9).

(2) In election, God is sovereign (9: 10-24).

(3) The blame of Israel's rejection rests upon herself (10).

Paul proceeds next (Rom. 11) to consider more carefully whether the historical facts do necessarily amount to a final, absolute rejection of Israel, and comes to the conclusion that they do not, again escaping from the unwelcome inference of the falsity of his Gentile gospel. This is the train of thought in chapter 11. The apostle speaks vehemently, confidently, and patriotically. ' I say then, Hath God cast away his people? God forbid.' Again Paul extracts comfort from the remnant doctrine — the elect within the elect; and finally his hope emerges triumphant: the now unbelieving race will one day be converted to Christianity, provoked to jealousy by the evangelization of the nations. ' It is God-worthy to be unchanging,' and on this firm foundation rest the great words, ἀμεταμέλητα τὰ χαρίσματα καὶ ἡ κλῆσις τοῦ Θεοῦ —the gifts and the calling of God are not repented of (Rom. 11: 29, RV mg.).

It is necessary to give this review of the passage, in order to get the right perspective for the usage of the predestinarian terms. The Jewish problem of a seeming cancelled election, according to the historical facts, leads Paul, using the same cycle of terms, to his strongest statement of the absolute sovereignty of God in the destiny of man. Let us select the vital phrases.

(1) Rom. 9: 11. ' For the children being not yet born, neither having done any good or evil, that the purpose of God according to election might stand, not of works, but of him that calleth ' — ἵνα ἡ κατ' ἐκλογὴν πρόθεσις τοῦ Θεοῦ μένῃ, οὐκ ἐξ ἔργων ἀλλ' ἐκ τοῦ καλοῦντος.

Jewish birth does not constitute heirship to the blessings of the covenant of grace. While Esau and Jacob were still in the womb and character unrevealed, Rebecca was told that the elder would serve the younger. Works, or merit, or character, have no preeminence in this ἡ κατ' ἐκλογὴν πρόθεσις but the sole origin is God Himself, ἀλλ' ἐκ τοῦ καλοῦντος. The divine call is again in its proper sequence, temporal and logical, and comes into the sphere of actual earthly life as the evidence of an eternal and purposive election.

(2) Rom. 9 : 16-18. ' You see, it is not a question of human will or effort, but of the divine mercy. . . . Thus God has mercy on anyone, just as He pleases and He makes anyone stubborn just as He pleases.' (C. H. Dodd.) Ἄρα οὖν οὐ τοῦ θέλοντος, οὐδὲ τοῦ τρέχοντος, ἀλλὰ τοῦ ἐλεῶντος Θεοῦ . . . ἄρα οὖν ὃν θέλει ἐλεεῖ, ὃν δὲ θέλει σκληρύνει.

Here Paul reveals that the election of God rests solely not upon *bare will* (as the term θέλω in preference to βούλομαι indicates) but upon merciful will, while mercy, apparently, cannot be conceived, apart from its pure negation, σκληρύνει. Hence, even the merciful disposition of God cannot be rightly apprehended, except through the conception of the absence of mercy from the divine character; the remarkable result being not unrighteousness but righteousness, an issue which Paul stoutly defends. If God shuts a man up to sin according to His good pleasure, who is man to accuse God of unfairness? Surely the Creator has unlimited rights over His creatures? This argument is enforced by the illustration of the potter and his clay.

(3) Rom. 9 : 22-24. ' Vessels of wrath . . . vessels of mercy.' Σκεύη ὀργῆς . . . σκεύη ἐλέους.

The vessels of wrath are the disobedient, with whom God is justly angry, and upon whom falls the Nemesis for sin. K. E. Kirk observes here (*Clarendon Bible*, p. 223), ' As S. Paul exempts God from responsibility for human sin, " fit " would give the sense better; he uses " fitted " (*i.e.* by God) as being the word which the predestinationist (who throws the responsibility on God) would naturally employ.' The point is that κατηρτισμένα εἰς ἀπώλειαν, to ease the problem of a decree of destruction, has been interpreted not ' fitted to destruction ' or ' made for eternal loss ' but ' fit or ripe or ready ' for destruction.

The vessels upon whom God has mercy are declared to be prepared beforehand for glory. The verb προητοίμασεν gives a very clear sense of pre-temporal action, but not so definite as foreknowledge or foreordination. It is to be noted that the parallel action relative to the vessels of wrath *has no reference to any eternal fitting to destruction.* The prefix is κατά, the intensive, not πρό the temporal. The two verbs in any case are different.

Καταρτίζω, to render ἄρτιος, *fit, complete,* means to furnish completely, equip, prepare. Here the past participle gives the sense of being *equipped* or *perfected.* In the passive sense we have also in the New Testament:

Luke 6 : 40. Κατηρτισμένος δὲ πᾶς ἔσται ὡς ὁ διδάσκαλος αὐτοῦ. ' But every one that is perfect shall be as his master.'

Hebrews 11 : 3. πίστει νοοῦμεν κατηρτίσθαι τοὺς αἰῶνας ῥήματι Θεοῦ. ' By faith we know that the worlds were prepared, made ready, or perfected by the word of God.'

2 Timothy 3 : 17. ἄρτιος only. ' That the man of God may be perfect, throughly furnished unto all good works.'

προετοιμάζω, √ ἕτοιμος, *prepared, ready* = *to be made ready* in the passive sense. Dalman (*The Words of Jesus,* p. 128) includes this verb amongst those which teach the sovereignty of God, and indicates that it is used equally for the destiny of the righteous and the wicked, as we read in Matthew 25 : 34 and 41.

(4) Rom. 11 : 2-5. ' God did not cast off his people whom he foreknew.' Οὐκ ἀπώσατο ὁ Θεὸς τὸν λαὸν αὐτοῦ ὃν προέγνω.

Here the very verb προέγνω, which we saw means ' personal contact or communion with ', demands that the import of τὸν λαὸν αὐτοῦ be not all Israel, but the remnant which is Israel's hope of future existence, the λίμμα κατ' ἐκλογὴν χάριτος, a spiritual Israel distinguished from the racial Israel, even in existence, ἐν τῷ νῦν καιρῷ. But this remnant is representative of all Israel, ὁ λαὸς τοῦ Θεοῦ, the people of God in the racial sense.

(5) Rom. 11 : 25, 26. ' A hardening in part hath befallen Israel, until the fulness of the Gentiles be come in; and so all Israel shall be saved.' Πώρωσις ἀπὸ μέρους τῷ Ἰσραὴλ γέγονεν. (ἡ πώρωσις, √ πῶρος, a stone = a covering with a callus.)

Here the agent of the hardening is not mentioned. It is merely an historical fact morally interpreted. Καὶ οὕτως πᾶς Ἰσραὴλ σωθήσεται, a conclusion which, together with the final utterance in his argument, is often made to imply Pauline universalism. Paul stands enthralled before the mystery of divine grace (verse 32), ' For God hath concluded them all in unbelief, that he might have mercy upon all.' Συνέκλεισεν γὰρ ὁ Θεὸς πάντας εἰς ἀπείθειαν, ἵνα τοὺς πάντας ἐλεήσῃ. It appears, however, that Paul's thought is still within the temporal sphere and he is envisaging a future from the ἐν τῷ νῦν καιρῷ of verse 5, until all Israel is saved. The remnant, in the hope of Paul, shall work as a leaven until the whole lump is leavened. A saved nation upon the earth is the vision of the apostle. He perceives that the bulk of the Jews, as history records, were committed to unbelief, although the remnant still held fast to faith, because destined to bring the whole nation back to God. Such was God's merciful providence and His amazing grace, working out salvation for the Jewish people in a manner confounding the mind of man.

THE PAULINE DOCTRINE

From Paul's vocabulary and its setting, it is possible to advance, somewhat, into his mind. A primary premise is that the apostle is not a theologian in the philosophical sense first of all, but pre-eminently a theologian in the experimental sense. All he knew of God and of His government of the world the apostle experienced, or arrived at, by revelation. Professor B. B. Warfield says (H.D.B., Vol. iii, p. 51), 'From the beginning to the end of his ministry, St. Paul conceived himself as the bearer of a message of undeserved grace to lost sinners, not even directing his own footsteps to carry the glad tidings to whom he would (Rom. 1: 10; 1 Cor. 4: 9; 2 Cor. 2: 12), but rather led by God in triumphal procession through the world, that through him might be made manifest the savour of the knowledge of Christ in every place — a savour from life unto life in them that are saved and from death unto death in them that are lost (2 Cor. 2: 15, 16).' Paul did not shape his doctrine of predestination into a perfect, logical system; indeed, he has left some things unexplained and irreconcilable, and his height of revelation reaches reverential awe and mystery, a worshipful attitude not in the presence of the terrible fate of the wicked, but of the merciful destiny of the righteous. Several elements of the apostle's teaching may be marked.

a. The remotest origin of predestination is the absolute sovereignty of God

In his thought, Paul equates the ideas of election and predestination, as we see from Ephesians 1 : 4, 5. God hath chosen us in Christ before the foundation of the world, having predestinated us. The two terms, ἐξελέξατο and προορίσας, are co-incident. It is true that, in post-Pauline theology, predestination is accepted as the wider term embracing ' whatsoever comes to pass ', all free and future acts of men and events contingent thereupon, as well as the salvation of men, which is the particular import of election. This all-inclusive predestination, cosmical, providential, national and individual, is entirely in harmony with the trend of both Old Testament and New Testament, but only in one case (1 Cor. 2 : 7, where we noted Beza translates by *praedefinio* in place of the usual *praedestinatio*) does Paul employ the term in reference to other than the salvation of individuals, *viz.* the gospel mystery or hidden wisdom. But there is a difference which the apostle makes and which is reflected in his choice of words, if the exegesis is sound. Election lays the emphasis upon the *persons* chosen, while predestination stresses what is the *design* of the delimitation, rather than the individuals themselves. This, we noted, was the bearing of the second accusative of προορίζω, while ἐκλέγω is a straightforward choice of some individuals out of a larger number.

Now this choice and design for the chosen have their source in the sovereign character of God, whose unchallengeable position as supreme in the affairs of men Paul defends as unquestionably righteous. It did not escape our notice that the term for *will*, θέλημα, which was Paul's favourite word, leads us away from the conception of pure will, or absolute determinism, or arbitrary despotism. The sovereignty of God is not a characteristic of stark naked volition alone, but of the complete and full personality of God. *It is not the will of God that elects and predestines, but God in His act of will.* ' Blessed be the God and Father of our

Lord Jesus Christ, who hath blessed us with all spiritual blessings in heavenly places in Christ: according as he (this same God and Father) hath chosen us in him . . . having predestinated us ' (Eph. 1: 3-5). Even when we come to the hardest statement of a high predestination in Romans 9-11, ' Jacob have I loved, but Esau have I hated ' (τὸν Ἰακὼβ ἠγάπησα, τὸν δὲ Ἠσαῦ ἐμίσησα) and ' I will have mercy on whom I will have mercy ', Paul was still speaking of the sovereign decrees of the God and Father of our Lord Jesus Christ, and not of a bare personified Will, irresponsible and unbalanced. He was engaging a perfect personality, defined in the Catechism of Westminister as ' a Spirit, infinite, eternal, and unchangeable, in his being, wisdom, power, holiness, justice, goodness, and truth '.

In a word, the ultimate origin of predestination is, in the Pauline theology, the God and Father of our Lord Jesus Christ. Paul is quite definite that upon nothing else save the sovereignty of God rests the decree of election. The idea of merit as the ground of choice is not for a moment entertained. Paul ousts it even with violence. Referring to Jacob and Esau, the children of Rebecca, the apostle says, ' For the children being not yet born, neither having done any good or evil, that the purpose of God according to election might stand, not of works, but of him that calleth ' (Rom. 9: 11). Merit could not be more completely excluded. Indeed, Paul can never bring into association the ideas of divine grace and human merit. In his thought, they are mutually exclusive, the one destroys the other. The failure to appreciate the Pauline background of free grace to a fallen race lies at the root of many misconceptions.

b. *Salvation is the first purpose of predestination, while service, as its crowning issue, proceeds from it*

This salvation is viewed by Paul in no narrow sense. In every passage where the apostle speaks of election, his conception of its goal is spacious. It is salvation through sanctification and faith envisaging a holy and enlightened life (2 Thes. 2: 13). It is salvation whose end is holiness, not man-made or earth-conceived, but ' according to his own purpose and grace ' (2 Tim. 1: 9). It is salvation which matures into kinship with God

and a growing likeness to our heavenly Father, ' unto the adoption of children by Jesus Christ to himself ' (Eph. 1 : 5).   It is
salvation, whose increasing and sure process, passing through foreknowledge, fore-ordination, calling and justification, reaches its
consummation in glorification (Rom. 8 : 30).   It is salvation
whose past is as great as its future.   Paul's kinsmen are Israelites
' to whom pertaineth the adoption, and the glory, and the cove-
nants, and the giving of the law, and the service of God, and the
promises; whose are the fathers, and of whom as concerning the
flesh Christ came, who is over all, God blessed for ever.   Amen '
(Rom. 9 : 4, 5).   It is salvation whose riches are still waiting full
release, ' that he might make known the riches of his glory on
the vessels of mercy, which he had afore prepared unto glory '
(Rom. 9 : 23).

It is impossible to deny, on Paul's view of salvation, the divine
interest in individual regeneration, and reformation, and perfection of personality.   We are not in the hand of God as mere
tools for the building of a kingdom of God.   Service is not the
cold design of election, whereby the units are mere cogs in a
great redemptive machine.   It is not easy to imagine the apostle
falling into raptures over the fact that he, and his fellow workers,
have been amazingly exploited for divine ends.   It was because
their own salvation came through, and was experienced by
service, that Paul was thrilled to find himself identified with the
divine purpose. One in heart and mind and will for the restoration
of the Jews, he could cry, ' O the depth of the riches both of the
wisdom and knowledge of God!' (Rom. 11 : 33).

Because service is both a factor and function of salvation we
find, in the Pauline literature, as was observed in the use of καλέω,
κλητός, and κλῆσις, a divine call to office, as well as to salvation.
But the apostle's soteriological viewpoint, that altruistic motives
spring from a converted personality, must be always borne in
mind.   It has been on the one hand the confusion of thought
regarding salvation and service, that has diluted the predestinarianism of Paul in later ages, while, on the other hand, a sane
view of both salvation and service has entered to relieve the strain
of an imagined arbitrariness in the destiny of men.   Beyond
doubt we are saved to serve; and nothing is plainer in the Pauline

theology, as born of his own experience, than that, in the heart
of all redemption, burns a missionary enterprise. The very first
letter Paul wrote (unless Galatians be so), contains an exultant
note about his Thessalonian converts, ' So that ye were ensamples
to all that believe in Macedonia and Achaia.   For from you
sounded out the word of the Lord . . . in every place ' (1 Thes.
1 : 7, 8).

c. Predestination is compatible with human responsibility
Paul does not appear to feel as intensely as we do the antinomy
between predestination and free will. This may be due to our
lapse from his premises. Paul did not allow the right of man to
challenge the mysterious ways of God. When the imagined
objector protests against the idea that God hardens whomsoever
He will and then brings to judgment for this same obduracy,
Paul replies, ' Nay but, O man, who art thou that repliest against
God? Shall the thing formed say to him that formed it, Why
hast thou made me thus?' (Rom. 9: 20). What the apostle
denies, however, is not really creative rights, but the claim to
reduce the decrees of God to the level of human comprehension.
The freedom of the will, again, may not be accepted in the
Pauline sense. Paul's assured presupposition is the ruin of man,
necessitating regeneration, and the will can only be absolutely or
ideally free when the nature is absolutely and ideally free from
sin. Yet relatively, freedom of will is not a delusion, for we act
according to our nature, whether that be good or evil, or as, in
the experience of Paul, our nature be divided, the good striving
for the mastery over the evil.

Paul's predestinarian scheme of things, when pushed to its
utmost, may be construed so as to ease the tension between
election and free will, by making the Creator responsible. But
this rather makes matters worse when we consider human responsibility. How can a man be held responsible for a life lived
according to the nature given to him by a sovereign Creator,
out of which nature, moreover, he is impotent to escape?
Paul does not flinch from maintaining that man is responsible, a
fact which excludes any interpretation of his doctrine in a spirit
of hyper-Calvinism. The other side of Paul's predestinarianism is

the accent upon human responsibility, and that is repeated in all his letters without apology or explanation, as if it were completely compatible with divine sovereignty.

This emphasis upon responsibility is upheld by several points:

(1) A very large part of the Pauline literature is devoted to moral exhortation. The apostle's readers are treated as intelligent agents who are conscious of ethical judgment. In the section Romans 9: 30 - 10: 13, Paul makes the Jews responsible for their own apostasy. They had the gospel nigh them in their mouth and in their heart, yet they stumbled at the stone of stumbling. Why? 'Because they sought it not by faith, but as it were by the works of the law' (9: 32).

(2) Paul conceives of grace, not as diminishing, but as increasing moral responsibility, e.g. Philippians 2: 12, 13, 'Work out your own salvation with fear and trembling. For it is God which worketh in you both to will and to do of his good pleasure.'

(3) Grace, which is the operation of divine sovereignty, may be frustrated, e.g. 2 Corinthians 6: 1, 'We then, as workers together with him, beseech you also that ye receive not the grace of God in vain,' a view taken entirely from the human side, disclaiming any fault on the divine side.

(4) Paul himself practises strenuous moral effort lest he forfeit his crown. He feels free to win or lose his soul, e.g. 1 Corinthians 9: 27, 'But I keep under my body, and bring it into subjection: lest that by any means, when I have preached to others, I myself should be a castaway.' Moreover, he strives after perfection, e.g. Philippians 3: 12-14, 'Not as though I had already attained . . . I follow after . . . I press toward the mark.'

Thus, it is evident that Paul held firmly by human responsibility in the very face of absolute divine sovereignty and without any consciousness of disparity. 'For we must all appear before the judgment seat of Christ; that every one may receive the things done in his body, according to that he hath done, whether it be good or bad' (2 Cor. 5: 10).

d. Predestination has a place for human redemptive co-operation
Absolute as the apostle may state the divine sovereignty to be,
he leaves room for human effort in the exercise of faith unto
salvation.   All students of Paul's theology in its full orbit have
noticed his preference for the preposition σύν, *with*, which he
prefixes to his verbs.   While the other New Testament writers
use μετά, Luke and Paul employ σύν. (*Vide* Abbott-Smith, p. 424.)
Again, we noted in the exegesis of 2 Thessalonians 2: 13, 14,
the union indicated by the one governing preposition ἐν between
the ministry of the Spirit, consequent upon the eternal election,
and the outgoing of the soul in belief of the truth.   In fact, Paul's
doctrine of faith, asserting its divine initiation in the human
soul, being a conscious motion towards Christ as Saviour, does
not allow us to neglect the part man must play in his own salvation.   If the apostle does trace this ability of saving faith to
an eternal decree, such predestination does not annul the individual consciousness of its operation in life.   It is true that he views
election as the guarantee in itself that it shall accomplish its
purpose, and he even brings this effectual grace down into the
temporal sphere with the assurance that He who has begun a
good work in the human soul will perfect it to the finish.   Yet all
this doctrine of perseverance in grace does not destroy, in his
preaching, the continual exhortation to increased effort in holy
living and in evangelical witness and service.   Some would even
argue that, in spite of Paul's high doctrine of predestination, he
taught, in unison with the sacred writer to the Hebrews, the
possibility of falling away, which raises the power of human
co-operation in its negative aspect to a dangerous height, and
may even be regarded as a *reductio ad absurdum* of divine
sovereignty.   The point here, however, is that no-one can deny
the room Paul has left for human redemptive co-operation in
his doctrine of predestination.

e. Predestination in relation to the destiny of the wicked
    includes reprobation
The most acute problem in the apostle's doctrine of predestination
is his reference to the fate of evil-doers, and his lack of precise
definition of their destiny.   Has Paul a doctrine of reprobation?

When we review the passages on the subject, the conclusion that the apostle certainly had some mind upon the question is unavoidable. The same verb παρέδωκεν, *hand over*, in Romans 1: 24, 26, 28, denotes mere abandonment and not determined, or even pre-determined, causation. The effective cause of divine desertion is pagan immorality. The word ἀδόκιμον, *reprobate, rejected*, is the negative of δόκιμον, *approved* or *that which can abide the test*. The disapproved, unable to pass the test, is worthless and hence rejected. We have three instances of the use of the term. (i) 2 Corinthians 13 : 5-7, where the test is the indwelling of Christ : ' Know ye not your own selves, how that Jesus Christ is in you, except ye be reprobates?' (ii) 1 Corinthians 9: 27, where the word is rendered by the AV as ' castaway ' : ' Lest that by any means, when I have preached to others, I myself should be a castaway,' meaning, lest Paul himself should stand disapproved before the judgment seat of Christ. The sense of moral responsibility is conspicuously present in this utterance of Paul and he is far from blaming God should he run his race to such an inglorious finish. That he was predestined to fail, is remote from the apostle's mind. (iii) Romans 1 : 28. Hence, in this third instance, ' God gave them over to a reprobate mind,' the meaning is that God abandoned the heathen to their own mind and a way of life entirely disapproved on any ethical test whatsoever. This idea of desertion involves also hopelessness of ever being able to pass the test, because the grace of God is removed.

From such reference to the destiny of the wicked, it is obvious that the apostle did express his mind upon the subject and held a doctrine of reprobation.

The question is, in what sense he believed that God came into relation with evil-doers. Certainly Paul inherited the high conception of sovereignty held by the Hebrew race, wherein everything is ultimately traced to a first Cause; but it is not so clear that he has stated a case for the positive damnation of the wicked, at least by the eternal counsel and fore-ordination of God. Let us examine this further.

(1) The idea of election, which he expresses by the verb ἐκλέγειν, presupposes a number, *massa perditionis*, out of which some are chosen to eternal life, and this election is pre-temporal

before such are born, and pre-determined before the character of
such is lived out in the earthly sphere.   The utter absence of a
deliberate and definite election to destruction in the same eternal
sense is marked.   There are no prefixes to suggest a plan beforehand.   The silence of Paul on this side does not argue that there
is no such positive decree, but it was not revealed to Paul, and it
was not his business to know.   He is content to remain in the
presence of a mystery, and his view is that it is a *mystery of
mercy*, that men have been saved from a just condemnation falling upon the whole race, and not a mystery of retribution.

(2)   The terms employed to describe reprobation indicate a
negative abandonment to the ill desert of the wicked's own evil
deeds.   They are deserted in their sin, and, while Paul may have
believed that saving grace was denied such, yet, at the same
time, he held them responsible for their sins and supremely
responsible for their rejection of the way of life, or, in the case of
the heathen, of the inner light of conscience, *i.e.* the innate moral
law.   In this he is in harmony with the teaching of the whole
New Testament, *e.g.* our Lord's lament over Jerusalem.   ' How
often would I . . . and ye would not ' (Mt. 23 : 37); and ' this is
the condemnation, that light is come into the world, and men
loved darkness rather than light, because their deeds were evil '
(Jn. 3 : 19).   That evil men work out their own destiny, while
good men are good by the mercy of God, is stated in the familiar
verse, ' The wages of sin is death; but the gift of God is eternal
life through Jesus Christ our Lord ' (Rom. 6 : 23).

(3)   Again there is, on the other hand, manifest preparation on
behalf of the elect, that grace might achieve its end.   The chosen
are borne along in a scheme of regeneration, sanctification and
glorification.   They are not elected on the chance that they will
be kept until the day of glory.   The means of grace are prepared
for their pilgrimage.   Like Paul, the redeemed are persuaded that
the Saviour is able to keep that which they have committed unto
Him till the good fight of faith is victoriously finished.   Paul, on
the other hand, has nothing to say of such parallel preparation
for the doomed, that they may unavoidably reap their destiny of
damnation.   It is impossible to conceive of God as perfect, if He
were to arrange for the commission of sin, whereby moral ruin

would be inevitable for some. However the Scripture may be interpreted, such a conclusion is unthinkable.

The most difficult passages are:

Romans 9: 18. ' Whom he will he hardeneth.'

The reference to Pharaoh takes us to the Old Testament, where it is significant to observe that the verb is used of the Egyptian king's own act, of the impersonal processes of law, and of the divine act as the source of every event in the Creator's universe. All this suggests that the hardening process is not a pre-determined plan of eternal positive decree, but is simply in accordance with the fixed operation of the ethical laws of the universe and of human nature.

Romans 9: 21-22. Vessels made ' unto dishonour . . . vessels of wrath fitted to destruction.'

Again there is the absence of pre-temporal arrangement in the case of those with whom God is righteously angry. The scene lies in the time-sphere and destruction is already shaping in the earthly life, for God is said to have endured such wrath-worthy persons with much long-suffering.

But the absolute sovereignty of God in relation to the wicked is not here easily dismissed. Competent attempts have been made to escape the divine responsibility for the making of the vessels of dishonour and wrath, *e.g.* C. H. Dodd takes the sense ' fit ', as we saw, rather than ' fitted ' for destruction, and this in a larger defence of the divine character. ' Although God is not responsible to human judgment, and we are not necessarily called to show that His action is guided by any principle but His own arbitrary will, yet actually a moral quality *can* be detected in His dealings, and that in two ways: (1) Although some men are objects of His anger (or rather are " objects of retribution ", 1 : 18), ripe and ready for destruction, yet these very men God has tolerated most patiently. The reference is to the forbearance of 3 : 25, the kindness, patience, and forbearance of 2 : 4. It is not indeed said here, as in 2 : 4, that His kindness is intended to lead its objects to repentance. The suggestion is rather that forbearance is no more than a stay of execution. But, in the light of 3 : 25, and of the conclusion in chapter 11, we may say that something more positive is really in Paul's mind. In any case, however, it is clear that there is something inherent in the character of God, which leads Him to show such forbearance, even to those who are not within the terms of His promise and covenant: (2) His plan must be judged not by its negative effect in excluding some men, but by its positive effect in securing untold blessings for the chosen: " He means to show the wealth that lies in His glory for the objects of His mercy." ' (*Moffatt's Commentary*, p. 159.)

Another essay to relieve the seemingly intolerable position, that God made some in order to damn them, is made by K. E. Kirk, ' St. Paul is very careful not to say that God has ever exercised, or will ever exercise, this right,' referring to the potter's creatorship. ' The argument is purely hypothetical: " If God were to do so, no-one could blame Him." In fact, by a judicious choice of language he suggests very forcibly that God never would emulate the potter and deliberately make a vessel of wrath, capable only of being destroyed. Of even the worst men it can only be said that they are " fitted for destruction ", not that they are doomed to it; and, in fact, God, so far from destroying them, " endures them with much longsuffering." Even in this grim discussion the Apostle avoids every phrase that could commit him to the doctrine of predestination to damnation.' (*Clarendon Bible*, p. 124.)

Romans 11: 7. ' The election hath obtained it, and the rest were blinded.'

The idea goes back to 9: 18, but a different verb is used. This hardening, blinding, or stupor is indicated to come from God, but, in the case of the Jews, it was temporary; or at least it was so in the case of the real representatives of the race. We would say that God overruled this obstinacy of the Jews for His own purposes of mercy.

Romans 11: 32. ' For God hath concluded them all in unbelief.'

This shutting up in the road to final unbelief was a direction caused by God, not that unbelief might bring doom, but, on the contrary, might hasten mercy. Also it is related by Paul as a fact in the history of the Jews, and is confined to God's dealing with His own people.

(4) Once again there is ample evidence in Paul's writings that

election is based upon experience but non-election is not. The witness of the early Church is to the great grace of God, but never to any consciousness of predestination to damnation, from which a repentant sinner felt he could not escape.

f. *Predestination is ' in Christ '*, ἐν Χριστῷ (Eph. 1 : 4; 2 Tim. 1: 9). This phrase emphasizes two characteristics of the Pauline theology — its Christocentric nature, and the idea of union or identification with Christ. These two are living traits of his thought. Thus Paul conceived predestination as ' in Christ ', so guarding his grasp of the truth from any rigour of impersonal will or monotheistic autocracy. The destiny of men is determined ' in Christ ', which indicates a relationship of humanity with Christ, whom Paul taught to be its Adamic head. Also the phrase points to a relationship of God with Christ, which Paul presented as Fatherhood. Some, indeed, would interpret more strongly as Fatherhood in covenant with the Son for human redemption.

g. Predestination glorifies God

Predestination, individual, national, or cosmical, directs to the poised perfection of the divine Being. Nothing in Paul's scheme lies outside the absolute sovereignty of God. God from all eternity did ordain ' whatsoever comes to pass ', even the actions of free and morally responsible beings. The apostle's interest, however, is in human redemption. The wider predestination is just the essential background of election, for, in the interests of personal salvation, nothing may exist beyond the reach of divine omnipotence, omniscience, and omnipresence.

The end of all the purposes of God is a purpose of infinite mercy. This unmerited grace toward mankind in their lost estate is the brightest element in the glory of God.

CONCLUDING THOUGHTS

It is now left for me to append some thoughts upon this doctrine of Pauline predestination, which are directed by later interpretations of the apostle's mind.

At the very outset it must be obvious that the unsystematic, and almost paradoxical, presentation of this truth, as a matter of experience rather than theology, does open the door to many, and contradictory, interpretations.   Whatever view, however, may be taken of some of the apostle's sayings, the general trend of his mind is unmistakable and in harmony with the rest of New Testament revelation.   The leading direction of Paul's thought is definitely predestinarian.

This sovereign view of Paul's teaching dismisses, first of all, any doctrine of *universalism*.   Some authorities do hold that the apostle's outlook upon life was that, in the end, all shall be saved. This interpretation is materially assisted by certain presuppositions, which are at variance with the Reformed Faith, *e.g.* the denial of the historicity and personality of the first man, Adam; the construction of the Fall as really an upward step in moral consciousness; the belief that the death of Christ was actually, and not merely potentially, sufficient for all men; the theory of election as only to service and never to salvation; and the doctrine of conditional immortality, wherein some win eternal life by spiritual contact with God, whereas others lose their souls by becoming atrophied through neglect, until existence itself ceases. It is not suggested that all such premises form the thought-background of all who sincerely hold this universalist interpretation of Paul's teaching, but almost invariably one or other of these tenets precedes the view.   The genuine altruism of all who accept the doctrine of universalism is to their eternal credit; but it is not true to experience, nor yet to the view-point of the whole New Testament.   It is undeniable that universalist texts may be found in the sayings of Christ or the writings of the apostles, or such, at least, as lend themselves to a universalist interpretation.   The purpose of these may be to warn against a heartless dogmatism or to humble us before the mystery of life.

Again, this Pauline predestination disagrees with the Arminian tradition, which consciously or unconsciously has entered into much of our modern theology.   Arminius (d. 1609) admitted, in the first place, only a general decree that God predestined all who should believe in Christ to salvation, rejecting an individual election with its infallible safeguards through life, until the consummation in glory is reached.   In the second place he was ready to accept a sort of election based upon foreknowledge. It was, in reality, a divine choice, not of particular souls, but of *special moral qualities*, the expression of which in character by certain individuals guaranteed their salvation. We have much of this teaching in our day, because much of it is true. Almost the earliest interpretation of Paul's mind upon the destiny of man, that of the Greek Fathers, was ' Conditional Predestination, *i.e.* election is a preordination of blessings or rewards for such as are foreseen to be up to a certain measure, worthy of them ' (G. P. Fisher, *History of Christian Doctrine*, pp. 165 f.).

This position refuses to distinguish between *common* grace, the operations of the Holy Spirit, universal in greater or lesser degree to all, and *efficacious* grace, which achieves its end in the conversion of the sinner. It is left to the moral ability of man to accept Christ and so escape eternal loss. The death of Christ is thus a fearful venture of God, uncertain as to its issue. On this view, God puts Himself at the mercy of something outside Himself, since the divine foreknowledge, supposed to be its safeguard, is merely contemplative and not executive.

Finally the interpretation of the teaching of Paul, as here outlined, is substantially that of Augustinianism, Calvinism, the *Westminster Confession of Faith*, and the Thirty-nine Articles.

The most rigid exponent, of course, is Calvin, who sets forth his view of positive reprobation in the eternal decree of damnation. Calvin was driven to this stern position by the sheer force of logic, as Paul was not, if our exegesis of the Pauline doctrine is correct. In the *Institutes* (*e.g.* Book iii, Ch. 24, 12) Calvin writes, ' Whom therefore He hath created unto the shame of life and destruction of death, that they should be instruments of His wrath and examples of His severity : from them, that they may come to their end, sometime He taketh away the power to hear His word, and sometime, by the preaching of it, He more blindeth and amazeth them.' Those who are proud to call themselves Calvinists do not follow the master-mind in this direction. Paul grounded election not upon the decrees of God as active will, but of God as our heavenly Father in Christ Jesus.

' Calvin is emphatic concerning the reprobate. Indeed, it is his uncompromising language on this side of the doctrine which

has been the rock of offence for so many, and there are still those
who would sum up Calvinism in some phrase about the doom of
the damned.   But the Reformer is merely following through with
his logic.   If we cannot assign any reason for God bestowing His
mercy on His people just as He pleases, so neither can we have
any reason for His rejecting others, save the Divine Will.   When
God is said to visit in mercy or harden whom He will, men are
reminded that they are not to seek for any cause beyond that
will.   There the finite mind has to leave it.'   (*Calvinism*, by
A. Dakin, p. 93.)

Writing upon the *Westminster Confession of Faith*, Dr. John
McConnachie says (*Evangelical Quarterly*),[1] ' The Confession is
assuredly right in giving an important place to God's Decree —
His plan of Salvation — which is the fundamental doctrine of
grace and the basis of all that follows — effectual calling, justification, etc.   But it took an unfortunate step in being led away in
its doctrine of Divine Sovereignty from the earlier insight of the
Scots Confession that predestination has to be interpreted through
Christology.   It is not apart from, or before Christ, but in Christ
that men's destinies are determined.   " For that same eternal
God and Father elected us in Christ Jesus, before the foundation
of the world and appointed Him to be our Head and Brother,
our Pastor and great Bishop of our souls " (*Scots Confession*,
art. viii).'   Like the *Scots Confession*, the Articles of the Church
of England, although also Calvinistic, omit any reference to a
pre-determined doom of the damned.

It is well to be clear upon this subject of Pauline reprobation
and a *decree of damnation* must be distinguished from it.   Let us
define reprobation in the words of Wm. Cunningham (*Reformers
and Theology of the Reformation*, p. 548) : ' Calvinists are careful
to distinguish between two different acts, decreed or resolved on
by God from eternity and executed by Him in time — the one
negative and the other positive, the one sovereign and the other
judicial — both frequently comprehended under the general
name of reprobation.

' (1)   *The negative or sovereign* — commonly called non-

---

[1] Vol. xvi (1944), p. 275.

election, preterition, or passing by — is simply resolving to leave
(and in consequence leaving) some men, those not chosen to
everlasting life, in their natural state of sin and misery — to
withhold from them or to abstain from conferring upon them
those supernatural gracious influences which are necessary to
enable any man to repent and believe; so that the result is that
they continue in their sin with the guilt of all their transgressions
upon their head.

'(2) *The positive or judicial* is more properly that which is
called, in the *Westminster Confession of Faith*, " foreordaining to
everlasting death " and " ordaining " those who have been passed
by " to dishonour and wrath for their sin ". God ordains no man
to wrath or punishment except on account of his sin; and makes
no decree, forms no purpose to subject any to punishment, but
what has reference to, and is founded on, their sin as a thing
certain and contemplated.

' But the first or negative act of non-election — preterition or
passing by — may be said to be absolute, since it is not founded
on sin and perseverance in it as foreseen. Sin foreseen cannot be
the proper ground, or cause, why some men are elected and others
are passed by, for all men are sinners and were foreseen as such.'

Again (p. 550): ' Calvinists maintain that, while the decree of
election is the cause or source of faith, holiness and perseverance
in all in whom they are produced, they hold that the preterition
of some men — *i.e.* the first or negative act in the decree of
reprobation based upon God's good pleasure, the counsel of His
Will — puts nothing in men, causes or effects no change in them,
but simply leaves them as it found them, in the state of guilt
and depravity to which they had fallen; while they admit that
the second or positive part of the decree of reprobation — the
foreordination to wrath and misery, as distinguished from preterition — is founded upon the foresight of men's continuance in
sin. God, in the purpose and act of preterition, took from them
nothing which they had, withheld from them nothing to which
they had a claim, exerted upon them no influence to constrain
them to continue in sin or to prevent them from repenting and
believing; and in further appointing them to dishonour and
wrath *for their sin*, He was not resolving to inflict upon them

anything but what He foresaw that they would then have
fully merited.'

Thus, later thought upon Pauline predestination definitely
refuses to hold that there exists any predetermined decree of
damnation and distinguishes such from Paul's doctrine of reprobation. That God created some to be doomed to everlasting
destruction before ever they were born and apart from their
character on earth finds no place either in the mind of Paul,
nor in the writings of the more recent of his interpreters. While
Calvin may have stepped aside in pursuing his relentless logic,
in positing a doctrine of damnation, and sacrificing instinctive
love to the necessities of an ideal system of theology, on the whole
his teaching is supremely Pauline. The lines of Burns in *Holy
Willie's Prayer* are a caricature of Calvin's extreme position :

> ' O Thou that in the heaven does dwell !
> Who, as it pleases best Thysel',
> Sends ane to heaven and ten to hell
>   A' for Thy Glory;
> And no for any guid or ill
>   They've done before Thee.'

While the problem of the fate of unbelievers, involving the
divine permission of sin, must always be hard for our finite
minds, the light granted to us in the Pauline corpus, and through-
out the whole New Testament, leads us to rest confidently in the
Fatherhood of God as revealed in His Son, our Saviour, Jesus
Christ. J. Gresham Machen (*The Christian View of Man*, p. 17),
in his published broadcasts to the American public on predestination, says, ' God only acts according to His nature. Never in
the very smallest of all His works will He depart, by one hair's
breadth, from that perfect standard which the perfection of His
own nature sets up. I think that is what one of my old teachers
meant, when he said, if I remember rightly his words, that God
is the most obligated being that there is. He is obligated by His
own nature. He is infinite in His wisdom, therefore He can never
do anything that is unwise; He is infinite in His justice, therefore
He can never do anything that is unjust; He is infinite in His

goodness, therefore He can never do anything that is not good; He is infinite in His truth, therefore it is impossible that He should lie.' Thus we rest, as we face destiny, upon the revealed character of God in all its moral perfection.

There is today, both by faith and reason, a consensus of belief that predestination, while beyond our ken completely to resolve, is a truth which serves the sense of human safety, since both good and evil are in God's almighty and loving hands. What predestination does not imply may be set forth with confidence.

Predestination does not mean, and Paul did not teach:

(1)   That God delights in damnation, or the second death.

(2)   That as the careers of the evil are foreordained, such are driven against their will to sin and to reject Christ, in order that their evil destiny may be fulfilled.

(3)   That election shuts the door against any who wish to enter in and be saved.

(4)   That any individual can declare himself to be non-elect, and give this as a reason for his immoral life or his rejection of Christ.

NEW TESTAMENT STUDIES

THE DEATH OF CHRIST

By JAMES DENNEY, D.D. Edited and Revised by Professor R. V. G. TASKER M A., D D.

In a most scholarly way the author analyses the references to the death of Christ in the synoptic Gospels, the early chapters of Acts, Paul's Epistles, Hebrews and the Johannine writings. He then shows the importance of the doctrine for preaching and theology. This edition includes part of his later book *The Atonement and the Modern Mind*, in which he considers some of the difficulties found in the doctrine by recent thinkers.

208 pp. 9s. 6d.

THE APOSTOLIC PREACHING OF THE CROSS

By the REV. LEON MORRIS, B.SC., M.TH., PH.D.

In this full-length work the author studies the great New Testament expressions used to describe what our Lord accomplished in His death, against their Old Testament and Rabbinic backgrounds. His aim is to show what our Lord and the apostles meant when they used such terms as ' redeem ', ' reconcile ', ' propitiate ', ' justify ', *etc*., and every important occurrence of these words is included in the survey. In addition a whole chapter is devoted to the meaning of the word ' blood ' in relation to our Lord's death. This is an important and scholarly work.

296 pp. 15s.

PAUL BEFORE THE AREOPAGUS

AND OTHER NEW TESTAMENT STUDIES

By Professor N. B. STONEHOUSE, D.D.

This book makes available to a wider circle of readers a number of important studies contributed by the author to theological journals or published in monograph form. *204 pp. 15s.*

Write for Catalogue to the Publishers
THE TYNDALE PRESS
39 BEDFORD SQUARE, LONDON, W.C.1

TYNDALE MONOGRAPHS

The Biblical Doctrine of Judgment
By the Rev. LEON MORRIS, B.SC., M.TH., PH.D., Warden of
Tyndale House, Cambridge.   72 pp.   5s.

Biblical Exegesis in the Qumran Texts
By Professor F. F. BRUCE, M.A., D.D., Rylands Professor of
Biblical Criticism and Exegesis in the University of Manchester.
                                            88 pp.   5s.

An Early Christian Confession
Philippians ii. 5-11 in Recent Interpretation
By the Rev. R. P. MARTIN, M.A., PH.D., Lecturer in Dogmatic
Theology, The London Bible College.   72 pp.   5s.

The Finished Work of Christ
By the Rev. A. M. STIBBS, M.A., Vice-Principal of Oak Hill
Theological College, London.   40 pp.   2s.

The Gospel in the Epistle to the Hebrews
By Professor R. V. G. TASKER, M.A., D.D., Professor Emeritus
of New Testament Exegesis in the University of London.
                                            56 pp.   2s.

The Meaning of the Word 'Blood' in Scripture
By the Rev. A. M. STIBBS, M.A., Vice-Principal of Oak Hill
Theological College, London.   *3rd Edition.* 32 pp.   1s. 6d.

Our Lord's View of the Old Testament
By the Rev. J. W. WENHAM, M.A., B.D., Vice-Principal of
Tyndale Hall, Bristol.   32 pp.   1s. 6d.

The Pastoral Epistles and the Mind of Paul
By DONALD GUTHRIE, B.D., M.TH., PH.D., Lecturer in New
Testament Language and Literature, The London Bible College.
                                            44 pp.   1s. 6d.

The Teacher of Righteousness in the Qumran Texts
By Professor F. F. BRUCE, M.A., D.D., Rylands Professor of
Biblical Criticism and Exegesis in the University of Manchester.
                                            36 pp.   2s.

Obtainable from any bookseller. Published by
THE TYNDALE PRESS
39 BEDFORD SQUARE, LONDON, W.C.1.